# Romantic Era Composers

Happy House

# About Wise & Wide

- A systematic 6-level English reading program based on Lexile® measures
- Diverse and interesting topics chosen from the elementary curriculums of Korea and English speaking western countries
- Well-written books in various forms including fiction stories, descriptive texts, and classics retold
- The informative but original fiction stories grab your interest, leading to the easy and clear understanding of the educational content.
- Improve thinking skills with solid after-reading activities at all levels of the series.

**Wise & Wide** is a 6-level English reading program that consists of 60 books and each level is systematically divided by Lexile® measures. The Lexile® Framework for Reading is the most popular reading measuring system in American formal education curriculums and many English programs. Over 20 out of 50 states in the U.S. mark Lexile® measures directly on students' final report cards and over 300 well-known publishers adopt and use Lexile® measures.

Experience many kinds of readings written by professional writers from the U.S. and England. They used interesting topics that were carefully chosen after analyzing elementary curriculums from around the world including Korea, the U.S., England, and Australia among many others. Comprehensive after-reading activities including graphic organizers, speaking tasks, and After-reading Tests are ready for you.

## Levels in the series and their corresponding Lexile® measures

| Level | Lexile® measures | U.S. Grade |
|-------|------------------|------------|
| Level 1 | Below 200L | Pre K - K |
| Level 2 | 190L - 400L | Lower Grade 1 |
| Level 3 | 350L - 530L | Upper Grade 1 |
| Level 4 | 420L - 650L | Grade 2 |
| Level 5 | 520L - 940L | Grade 3 - 4 |
| Level 6 | 830L - 1070L | Grade 5 - 6 |

\* Smart Readers: Wise & Wide level 1 is applicable to the preschool level in the U.S.

\* The source of the relationship between Lexile® measures and U.S. school grades: CCSS(Common Core State Standards) FOR ENGLISH LANGUAGE ARTS, APPENDIX A (2012, which is used by 45 states in the U.S.)

# Topic List

| | Level 1 | Level 2 | Level 3 | Level 4 | Level 5 | Level 6 |
|---|---|---|---|---|---|---|
| **Book 1** | Science>Biology: The hibernation of animals Story | Science>Biology: Living and nonliving things Story | Science>Biology: Animals & the Environment: Sea otters Story | Environment> Living with nature: The diver & the persimmon tree Story | Science>Biology: Animal: Amazing animals of the Amazon Story | Science>Biology: Germs, transmitted diseases Story |
| **Book 2** | Literature> World classics: Aesop's fables Story | Literature> Traditional fairy tale: Old tales about stones Story | Social Studies> Economy: To run a business to make and save money Story | Science>Biology> Plants: Photosynthesis Story | Science>Earth science: Earth's layers, earthquakes, volcanoes, and earth's atmosphere Report | Mathematics> Sequence: The golden ratio & the Fibonacci sequence Story |
| **Book 3** | Science>Physics: How shadows are formed Story | Literature> World classics: Peter Pan Story | Science>Scientific technology: Nanobots Story | Literature>Myths: World's creation stories Story | Literature> Legend: The story of King Arthur Story | Literature>Myths: Constellation myths Story |
| **Book 4** | Literature> Traditional literature: The Talmud Story | Science>Biology> Animal: Polar bears Story | Science>Biology> Animal: Mountain gorillas Story | Social Studies> Cultural anthropology: Amazing ancient cultures of the world Story | Science> Earth science: Clouds and weather Story | Literature> Human & animals: The friendship between a girl and a horse Story |
| **Book 5** | Social Studies> Ethics: Rules in daily life Story | Science>Biology: The five senses Report | Social Studies> Cultural anthropology: Astonishing festivals Report | Art>Music: Stories from two operas Story | Social Studies> World culture & history: The Renaissance Story | Sports> Board sports: Surfing & snowboarding Story |
| **Book 6** | Social Studies> World geography & travel: Tourist attractions around the world Story | Science>Biology> Animal: Dinosaurs Story | Science> Astronomy: The solar system Story | Social Studies> People: Three great people who overcome hardships Story | Science>Scientific technology: The wonderful world of robots Report | Art>Music: Composers of the Romantic Era Report |
| **Book 7** | Science> Space science: The life of astronauts Report | Social Studies> Cultural anthropology: Mythological monsters from around the world Report | Mathematics> Elementary mathematics: Numbers, measurement, shapes and data Report | Science & Social Studies> Technology & culture: Inventions from around the world Report | Art>Works of art: Famous paintings Report | Social Studies> Human & animals: Animals in action for human Report |
| **Book 8** | Social Studies> Cultural anthropology: Various living cultures of the world Story | Art>Music: Instruments in the orchestra Story | Social Studies> Life safety: Learning and using outdoor survival skills Story | Social Studies> History: The California Gold Rush Report | Social Studies & Science> Psychology: Psychology in everyday life Story | Literature> World classics: The Merchant of Venice Story |
| **Book 9** | Social Studies> Jobs: Interviews about jobs Report | Science>Scientific technology: Developments in technology in different times Story | Social Studies> Politics>Election: Running for 3rd grade class president Story | Literature> World classics: Stories of Sherlock Holmes Story | Literature> World classics: Adrift in the Pacific Story | |
| **Book 10** | | Sports>Winter sports: Various aspects of some Winter Olympic sports Report | | | | |

* 10 books in each level will be published.

# How to Use
# This Book

## •Before Reading

You can easily find the topic and what kind of story you are about to read.

## •The text

All the stories were written by professional writers from the U.S. and England, so you will read authentic and appropriate English sentences and expressions in every book in the series.

## •Pop Quiz

Check out right away if you understand what you have just read by solving a pop quiz that checks your comprehension.

## •Key Words

The key words and expressions on each page are listed for you to easily study them.

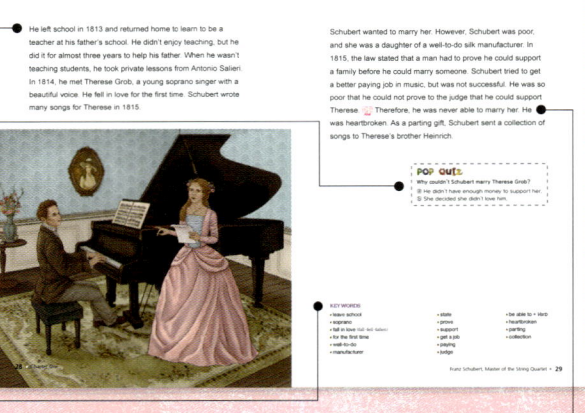

## •Aha! Tips

Download free Korean explanations at *www.ihappyhouse.co.kr* for all of the sentences marked with "Aha!". These explain cultural, scientific, and economic knowledge or they deal with aspects of English such as grammatical structures or idiomatic expressions. There are lots of "Aha! Tips" to help you understand the text.

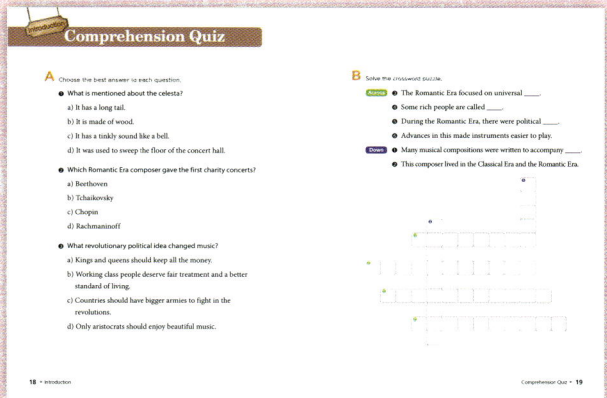

●**Comprehension Quiz**

After reading one chapter, solve various questions to find out if you fully understand the content.

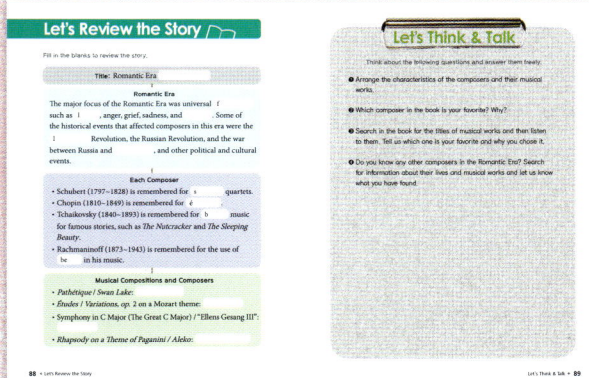

●**Let's Review the Story /**
●**Let's Think & Talk**

Fill in the blanks in the organizer to summarize the whole story. Express your own thinking and feelings about the story by answering the questions. You can build up logic and reasoning skills for your essay examinations in the future.

## Appendix

### Audio CD

In the CD audio book form, the texts are read vividly by American professional voice actors. (MP3 files downloaded for free)

### After-reading Test

Solve an additionally provided After-reading Test for each book.

### The Korean translation, Answer Keys, a Word Quiz, a Word List, and Aha! Tips for each book

You can download them for free at *www.ihappyhouse.co.kr* or *www.darakwon.co.kr*

# Before Reading

## Romantic Era Composers

Level 6–6,
Lexile® 980L

•Art›Music
•Report

## Classical Music from the Romantic Era: Emotional music with less structure and order

Romanticism is a style in the arts including music that originated in Europe toward the late 18th century. During the Romantic Era, not only nobles but also ordinary people had more opportunities to enjoy music thanks to the Industrial Revolution. Unlike earlier classical music which emphasized repetition and formality, classical music in the Romantic Era emphasized expressing people's subjective feelings lyrically and freely. In general, more powerful and more magnificent music appeared in the Romantic Era thanks to the development of various musical instruments. In addition, lieder became one of the fields in classical music and titles and explanations started to be added to symphonies.

In the book, we will check out famous composers who were very active in the Romantic Era. It will be a good opportunity for you to understand classical music better so that you will be more interested in it.

## Summary

Music from the Romantic Era that expresses various emotions through music developed greatly due to the political, economic, and social changes brought about by the Industrial Revolution, the French Revolution, and other historic movements. Some of the composers who made music in this era were Schubert, Chopin, Tchaikovsky, and Rachmaninoff. They are geniuses who overcame difficulties in their lives to give us beautiful music.

Schubert was the master of the string quartet who composed the famous *Marche Militaire in D Major* and variations on "Death and the Maiden." Chopin was a piano genius that composed beautiful piano music including an étude that almost all students who learn how to play the piano practice. In addition, Tchaikovsky composed various music for ballets such as *The Nutcracker, Swan Lake*, *The Sleeping Beauty*, etc. as well as other famous compositions such as *Pathétique*. Finally, Rachmaninoff was another musical genius who composed various pieces such as operas and a cappella songs besides a choral symphony called *The Bells* based on an Edgar Allan Poe poem.

# Contents

# Romantic Era Composers

# Romantic Era Composers

# The Passionate Romantic Era

Romantic is a word that has many meanings, but usually when people hear the word, they think of feelings. This is exactly what the Romantic Era of music is all about. The music deals with emotions, expressing passion and joy, spiritual ideas, and supernatural. It focuses on universal feelings such as love, anger, grief, sadness, and joy.

### KEY WORDS

- **passionate** (*cf.* passion)
- **era**
- **what ~ is all about**
- **deal with** (deal-dealt-dealt)

- **express**
- **spiritual**
- **supernatural**
- **focus on**

- **universal**
- **grief**

The Romantic Era of music is an important period in music history, because during this time many new forms of music were created. This was a time in history when composers left behind the restraints of classical music and began writing music that was more inventive and original. The era is debated, but the most common references say the Romantic Era lasted from the late 1780s to the early 1900s. Many composers, as you will see in this book, wrote their music to accompany popular poems and stories of the same time period. Art, literature, and drama were the basis for many of the famous compositions of this time. Some of the music is even spooky and gives the feeling of ghosts and other supernatural things. Other music developed around the theme of nature, as in storms and the seasons. Some music reflects strong feelings of love and heartbreak.

**KEY WORDS**

- period
- composer
- leave behind (leave-left-left)
- restraint
- classical
- inventive
- original

- debate
- common
- reference
- last
- accompany
- basis
- composition

- spooky
- develop
- around
- theme
- as in
- reflect
- heartbreak

The Industrial Revolution was rapidly changing the world at this time. Advances in industry and technology allowed musical instruments to be made differently, and made some easier to play. The piano became more popular, because the strings could be made longer and stronger. The foot pedals were added, and the piano was made bigger, giving it a better sound. New instruments were designed, such as the celesta, a clavier that makes a tinkly bell sound. To enjoy the new music better, orchestras became larger, adding more instruments and more types of instruments. For most Romantic Era composers, bigger was better when it came to orchestras.

▲ celesta
(When you hit the keyboard, a small hammer connected to the keyboard hits a metal plate and it makes a bell sound.)

**KEY WORDS**

- Industrial Revolution
- rapidly
- advance
- industry
- instrument

- string (*cf.* the strings)
- foot pedal
- add
- celesta
- clavier

- tinkly
- orchestra
- when it comes to

Up until the 1800s, only kings, queens, and rich people called aristocrats enjoyed performances of classical music and literature. Royals and aristocrats learned about classical music in their educations. They thought only people privileged enough to have such an education should enjoy classical music. So most concerts were private, and only certain people were allowed to attend.

**KEY WORDS**

- up until
- aristocrat
- royal
- privilege
- private
- attend

During the Romantic Era, that all changed. Political revolutions happened in which people of the working class demanded fair treatment and a better standard of living. There was the French Revolution, the war between Russia and Poland, the Napoleonic Wars, the Civil War in America, and the Spanish-American War. 🌐 People all over the world wanted change. They didn't think it was fair that aristocrats had almost all of the money. They also disagreed that only aristocrats should enjoy beautiful music. Romantic composers in Europe began giving the first public concerts in theaters and opera houses, and anyone could attend if they paid for a ticket. Some of the first charity concerts were given by Frédéric Chopin.

**KEY WORDS**

- political
- working class
- demand
- fair
- treatment
- standard of living

- the Napoleonic Wars
- the Civil War
- the Spanish-American War
- disagree (↔ agree)
- public
- charity

▲ a painting that shows the French Revolution, *Liberty Leading the People*

The Romantic Era composers looked at the world around them and translated their feelings about it into music. Composers looked to paintings, literature, drama, religion, and nature for their inspiration. Some of the inspirations expressed intense feelings and even fantasies. They began experimenting with new forms of music and they wanted to share them with the world.

Ludwig van Beethoven, one of the most famous composers of all time, lived in both the Classical Era and the Romantic Era. You might say he had the best of both worlds. He began writing music in the Classical Era, and by the time he died, he and Franz Schubert were composing Romantic Era music. Franz Schubert was one of the most prolific composers of the Romantic Movement. He created over 1,000 pieces of music and led the way for other Romantic Era composers.

▲ Ludwig van Beethoven

▲ Franz Schubert

Other famous composers of this era include Gustav Mahler, Johannes Brahms, Hector Berlioz, Richard Wagner, Franz Liszt, and Giuseppe Verdi. You may want to listen to some of their music and see what feelings it brings out in you. Much of the Romantic Era music is about feelings!

In this book, you will read about Schubert and three more Romantic Era composers and what inspired them to create beautiful music. These four composers span the musical period from the beginning to the end. Therefore, if you listen to their music, you will gain an understanding of the music from the entire Romantic Era. If you enjoy this music, there are many more Romantic Era composers to learn about.

**KEY WORDS**

- translate
- look to
- inspiration (cf. inspire)
- intense
- fantasy
- experiment
- of all time
- have the best of (have-had-had)
- prolific

- the Romantic Movement
- piece
- lead the way (lead-led-led)
- bring out (bring-brought-brought)
- span
- gain
- understanding
- entire

# Comprehension Quiz

**A** Choose the best answer to each question.

**❶** What is mentioned about the celesta?

a) It has a long tail.

b) It is made of wood.

c) It has a tinkly sound like a bell.

d) It was used to sweep the floor of the concert hall.

**❷** Which Romantic Era composer gave the first charity concerts?

a) Beethoven

b) Tchaikovsky

c) Chopin

d) Rachmaninoff

**❸** What revolutionary political idea changed music?

a) Kings and queens should keep all the money.

b) Working class people deserve fair treatment and a better standard of living.

c) Countries should have bigger armies to fight in the revolutions.

d) Only aristocrats should enjoy beautiful music.

# B Solve the crossword puzzle.

**Across**

❸ The Romantic Era focused on universal _____.

❹ Some rich people are called _____.

❺ During the Romantic Era, there were political _____.

❻ Advances in this made instruments easier to play.

**Down**

❶ Many musical compositions were written to accompany _____.

❷ This composer lived in the Classical Era and the Romantic Era.

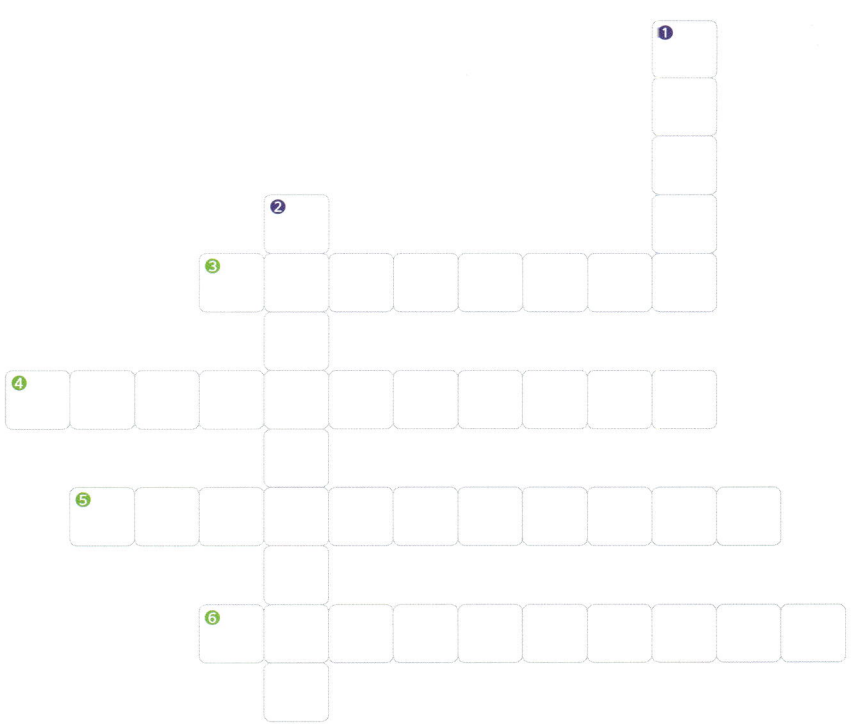

# Franz Schubert, Master of the String Quartet

Franz Schubert was born at the beginning of the Romantic Era of music on January 31, 1797, in Vienna, Austria. This city was well known for being a center of classical music. His father was a schoolmaster and his mother had worked as a housemaid before she married. Franz was one of fourteen children! His family was not rich, but his father made sure he received a good education.

First, he went to his father's school to learn to read, write, and do math; then he would go to music lessons. His father taught him the violin and his brother taught him the piano. The family loved music, and Franz wrote his first string quartet at the age 13 for him, his father and brothers to play together. 🌐

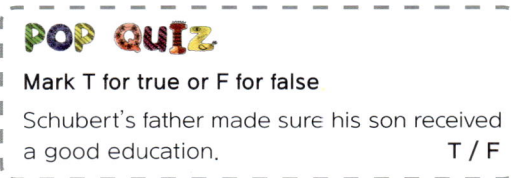

**POP QUIZ**

Mark T for true or F for false

Schubert's father made sure his son received a good education.                     T / F

**KEY WORDS**

- master
- string quartet
- Vienna

- be well known for
- schoolmaster
- housemaid

- make sure
- receive
- do (do-did-done)

These family members were a musical quartet, and Franz played the viola, which is larger than the violin. His two brothers played first and second violin. His father played the violoncello. As you can see, the names of these instruments all start with the letters viol, and they are all members of what is called the violin family. All these instruments are wooden, have four strings, and are played with a bow.

The violoncello is also called a cello, and it is the largest and deepest of the instruments. It has a pin on the bottom that looks like a stick and holds the violoncello off the floor. The viola is tuned an octave higher than the cello, but lower than a violin. It is the middle instrument in the family. The violin is smaller than the cello and the viola, and the music it plays is higher than the viola. In a musical piece, the first violin usually plays the melody, and the second violin usually plays harmony or a complementary rhythm.

**KEY WORDS**

- viola
- violoncello (= cello)
- what is called
- wooden
- bow
- largest

- deepest
- pin
- bottom
- tune
- octave
- musical piece

- melody
- harmony
- complementary
- rhythm

Franz Schubert continued to write and play chamber music his whole life. His string quartets are still considered some of the best of any of the Romantic Era composers. However, Schubert's family wasn't rich, and the instruments they played on weren't the best. Sometimes Franz would go to a local music warehouse so he could practice on better quality instruments than they had at home.

He also sang in the church choir, and when he was only seven years old, a man named Antonio Salieri recognized that he had great vocal talent. 🌐 Since Salieri was a prominent man in Vienna's musical world, he helped Franz Schubert get a choir scholarship for the Imperial Seminary called Stadtkonvikt. He began going to school there in 1808 and learning about the opera and the classical symphonic music of Mozart and Haydn.

**KEY WORDS**

- chamber music
- consider
- local
- warehouse
- choir
- recognize
- vocal
- talent
- since
- prominent
- get a scholarship (get-got-gotten)
- imperial
- seminary
- symphonic

▲ chamber music

(a form of classical music played by musicians with only a few musical instruments
that can all fit into the residence of a monarch or a noble)

▲ symphonic music

(music made for orchestral music)

While at Stadtkonvikt, he met another student named Joseph von Spaun, and they became good friends. Since Schubert was too poor to buy paper to write his music on, Spaun bought it for him. 📖 With a steady supply of paper, Schubert created his first orchestra and chamber music, symphonies, and several songs for the piano. His early choir lessons at the church influenced his music and he wrote many religious choral works. He continued to take private lessons from Salieri, and sometimes he even conducted the Stadtkonvikt orchestra while he was still a teenager! During this time, he made many lifelong friends including a rich man named Franz von Schober. These friends helped promote his music.

## POP QUIZ

**What did von Spaun do for Schubert?**

ⓐ He loaned Schubert pencils and pens.
ⓑ He bought Schubert paper so he could write music.

**KEY WORDS**

- steady
- supply
- influence
- religious
- choral

- work
- conduct
- lifelong
- including
- promote

- wind
- octet
- major (↔ minor)
- D
- in one's honor

Schubert's mother died in 1812. He began to write Wind Octet in F Major, D. 72 in her honor, but never finished it. A wind octet is written for eight instruments that are played using the breath, such as horns, bassoons, oboes, and clarinets. As in the quartet, the different instruments play their own parts.

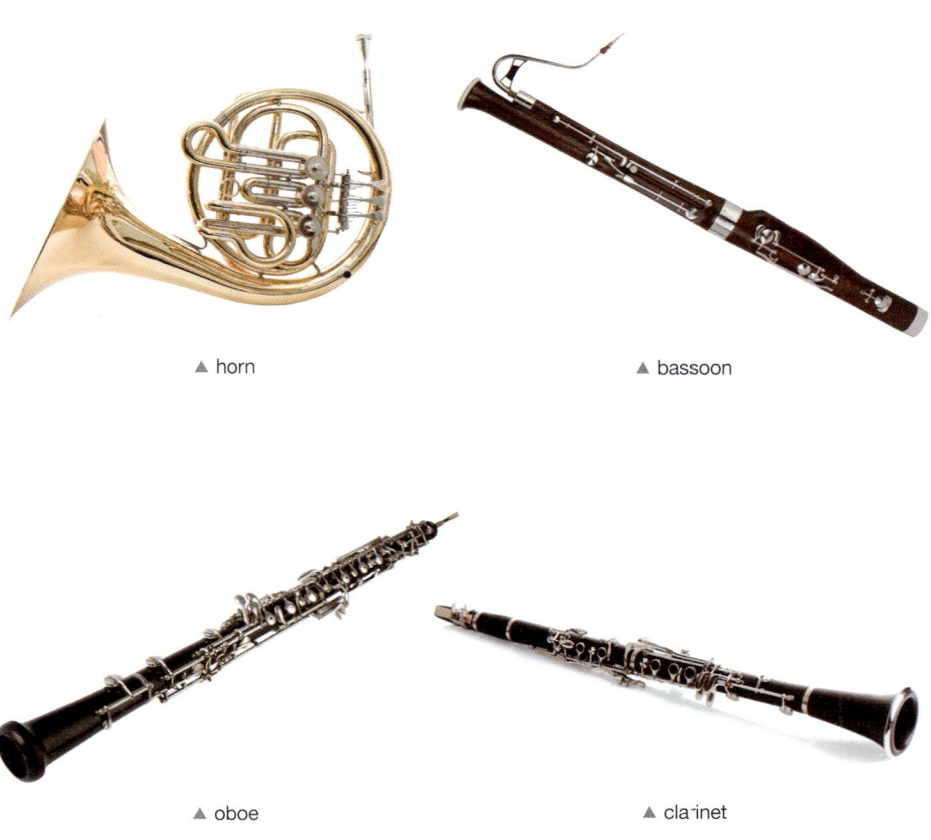

▲ horn

▲ bassoon

▲ oboe

▲ clarinet

He left school in 1813 and returned home to learn to be a teacher at his father's school. He didn't enjoy teaching, but he did it for almost three years to help his father. When he wasn't teaching students, he took private lessons from Antonio Salieri. In 1814, he met Therese Grob, a young soprano singer with a beautiful voice. He fell in love for the first time. Schubert wrote many songs for Therese in 1815.

Schubert wanted to marry her. However, Schubert was poor, and she was a daughter of a well-to-do silk manufacturer. In 1815, the law stated that a man had to prove he could support a family before he could marry someone. Schubert tried to get a better paying job in music, but was not successful. He was so poor that he could not prove to the judge that he could support Therese.  Therefore, he was never able to marry her. He was heartbroken. As a parting gift, Schubert sent a collection of songs to Therese's brother Heinrich.

## POP QUIZ

**Why couldn't Schubert marry Therese Grob?**

ⓐ He didn't have enough money to support her.
ⓑ She decided she didn't love him.

**KEY WORDS**

- leave school
- soprano
- fall in love (fall-fell-fallen)
- for the first time
- well-to-do
- manufacturer

- state
- prove
- support
- get a job
- paying
- judge

- be able to + *Verb*
- heartbroken
- parting
- collection

In 1816, Franz von Schober invited Schubert to come live with him. Schubert quit teaching at his father's school and accepted his friend's invitation. He threw himself into composing music, one piece after another, for an entire year. By now he had written hundreds of lieder, which are German songs for one person to sing with the piano. He also wrote many pieces for the orchestra and church choir.

Schubert's friends promoted his work by having parties called Schubertiades.  At the parties, Schubert's music was played, and people sang, danced, and read poetry. These parties made him popular in the Viennese musical circles.

**KEY WORDS**

- quit (quit-quit-quit)
- accept
- throw oneself into (throw-threw-thrown)
- lieder
- Viennese
- circle

Even though Schubert was gaining popularity, he still had to make money somehow. He went back to teaching with his father in 1817. Then, in 1818, he had a stroke of luck when he became the private music teacher to the family of Count Johann Karl Esterházy. The pay was good, and he was able to live in their fine house. He spent his days teaching singing and dancing to the Count's two young daughters, Marie and Karoline. All his spare time he spent writing music. He wrote piano duets for the two girls. One of these duets he turned into a world-famous composition called *Marche Militaire in D Major.* He wrote another duet called *Fantasie in F Minor* in 1828, and dedicated it to his beautiful young pupil, Countess Karoline.

## POP QUIZ

**Mark T for true or F for false.**

Schubert dedicated *Fantasie in F Minor* to Countess Karoline.　　T / F

**KEY WORDS**

- popularity
- somehow
- go back to (go-went-gone)
- a stroke of luck

- count
- spare time
- duet
- dedicate

- pupil
- countess

In 1819 and 1820, Schubert wrote more religious music and cantatas, which are sung and accompanied by instruments. Schubert loved the opera, and in the 1820s, he wrote over twenty operas and stage productions. One of them, *Fierrabras*, had over 1,000 pages of written music. None of them was successful.

In 1825 he took a trip to Austria, and while he was there he wrote a cycle of seven songs based on Walter Scott's *Lady of the Lake*.  This poem tells the story of a struggle between King James V of Scotland and James Douglas, Earl of Bothwell.

▲ The lake in *Lady of the Lake* is Loch Katrine in Sterling, Scotland.

The seven songs include one choral piece called "The Boat Song," which begins with the line, "Hail to the Chief." There are also three solo pieces called the Ellen songs. They were named after the Earl of Bothwell's beautiful daughter. "Ellens Gesang III" begins with the words, "Ave Maria," so people began calling it Schubert's "Ave Maria."  Ave Maria is the traditional Hail Mary prayer used by the Catholic Church. At some point, people stopped singing the words written by Walter Scott and replaced them with the Hail Mary prayer. This is the version most people hear today.

---

**POP QUIZ**

What is "Ellens Gesang III" from Schubert's cycle of seven songs sometimes called?

ⓐ Ave Maria
ⓑ The Boat Song

---

**KEY WORDS**

- cantata
- stage
- production
- cycle
- be based on
- struggle

- earl
- hail
- chief
- solo
- name after
- Gesang

- Ave Maria
- Hail Mary
- prayer
- the Catholic Church
- replace

He also wrote the Piano Sonata in A Minor, D. 845 in 1825. It is the beginning of the Symphony in C Major, D. 944, which is also called The Great C Major. He completed the symphony in 1826. In fact, he was always writing music! He greatly admired Ludwig van Beethoven, but he never thought he could be as good a composer as the great musician. 📖Aha! Schubert's Symphony in C Major, D. 944 sounds a little like some of Beethoven's music. When Beethoven died in 1827, Schubert was a torchbearer at his funeral.

Franz Schubert was not a show-off, and he didn't brag about what he was doing. He would play his music for his friends at the Schubertiades. But in public, he played other composers' musical compositions.

**KEY WORDS**

- sonata
- complete
- greatly
- admire
- torchbearer

- show-off
- brag
- in public
- variation
- maiden

- melancholic
- gloomy
- originally

Finally, in 1828, when he was thirty-one years old, Schubert gave a concert of his own works, which included the famous String Quartet in D Minor, D. 810 with variations on "Death and the Maiden." This is a melancholic — dark and gloomy — but beautiful quartet based on some of his earlier work. He originally wrote the music when he was sick and the music gives the feeling of death being near. He also played the Piano Sonata in G Major, also known as *Fantasie in G*. This was the only time he played his own music in concert.

Later that year Schubert began to feel ill, and his last pieces that he wrote reflect a quieter, even sad tone. In the summer, he became very ill with headaches, swollen joints, and a fever. He wasn't able to eat and keep food down. In November, he wrote his last letter to his friend Franz von Schober. He also had one final visit with Josef von Spaun. Before Schubert died on November 19, 1828, he asked to be buried next to Beethoven, who had died the previous year. His friends and family made sure that he was laid to rest near the famous composer. Rumors said the cause of his death was typhoid fever, but no one really knows for sure what disease cut this gifted composer down in the prime of his life. He was only thirty-one years old. Schubert's many friends held two concerts to raise money to place a monument over his grave. The concerts were successful, and a beautiful monument and bust of Schubert now marks his grave.

**KEY WORDS**

- headache
- swollen
- joint
- **keep down** (keep-kept-kept)
- bury
- previous
- lay to rest
- rumor
- typhoid fever
- disease
- **cut down** (cut-cut-cut)
- gifted
- prime
- **hold** (hold-held-held)
- raise
- place
- monument
- grave
- bust
- mark

▲ from the top left: the graves of Beethoven, Mozart, and Schubert

# Comprehension Quiz

**A** Choose all statements that describe a cello.

a) one of the violin family

b) larger than the viola

c) tinkly sound

d) deeper tone than the violin

**B** Mark T for true or F for false.

❶ Franz von Schober helped Schubert to get a scholarship to the Imperial Seminary Stadtkonvikt.　T　F

❷ When Schubert's mother died, he began to write Wind Octet in F Major, D. 72 in her honor.　T　F

❸ Schubert was a torchbearer at the funeral of Beethoven.　T　F

❹ Schubert's friends held concerts to raise money and placed a monument over his grave.　T　F

**C** Choose the best answer to each question.

❶ What musical composition did Schubert dedicate to Karoline, the daughter of Count Johann Karl Esterházy?

a) *Marche Militaire in D Major*

b) *Fantasie in F Minor*

c) *Lady of the Lake*

d) "The Boat Song"

❷ What happened to Schubert after he gave a concert of his own works?

a) He became famous and moved to London.

b) He received offers to take a concert tour in Europe.

c) He became ill with headaches, swollen joints, and a fever.

d) He had a big party with his friends.

❸ Why do you think Schubert asked to be buried next to Beethoven?

a) He admired Beethoven and thought he was a great composer.

b) Beethoven and Schubert were rivals.

c) Schubert thought he was better than Beethoven.

d) Beethoven gave a cemetery plot to Schubert.

# Frédéric Chopin, the Poet of the Piano

Do you play the piano? Like other instruments, the piano takes many hours of practice to master. If you are a student of the piano, your teacher may have had you practice with a piece of music called an étude. Chances are Frédéric Chopin wrote that piece of music.

Chopin was born in Poland sometime in early 1810. His birth date is surrounded in a bit of mystery. But the most unusual story about Frédéric Chopin is what happened to him after he died. His body was buried in two places!

Chopin said he was born on March 1, 1810, but his baptism certificate says he was born on February 22, 1810. He was born in a small village in the Duchy of Warsaw, Poland. Chopin was the second of four children. His father was a Frenchman, and he taught French language and literature at a school called the Warsaw Lyceum.

Frédéric began taking music lessons at a very young age. By the time he was seven years old, he was already being called "Little Chopin" and compared to the musical genius Wolfgang Amadeus Mozart. He played at concerts for rich people and he also played at public charity concerts. When he was twelve, his music teacher could not give him any more lessons, because Chopin was already more advanced in music than his teacher!

**KEY WORDS**

- étude
- (the) chances are (that)
- surround
- a bit of
- baptism
- certificate
- duchy
- Warsaw
- Lyceum
- compare to
- advanced

From 1823 to 1826, when Chopin was thirteen to sixteen years old, he attended school at the Warsaw Lyceum where his father worked. He spent his summer holidays on the estates of his friends in the country. This is where he first heard folk music and saw folk dancing. Chopin enjoyed this music and he began writing down the songs and the musical notes.

Back at school, Chopin continued writing new music. He wrote concertos for the piano, nocturnes, which are dreamy pieces that make you think of night, waltzes, which were often used as dance music, and mazurkas, which are dances inspired by the Polish folk music he heard during his summer holidays.

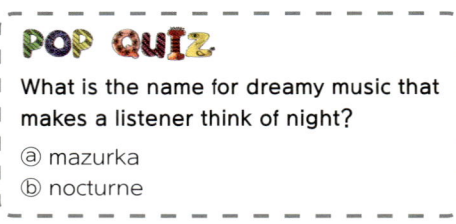

POP QUIZ

What is the name for dreamy music that makes a listener think of night?
ⓐ mazurka
ⓑ nocturne

### KEY WORDS

- estate
- folk
- **write down** (write-wrote-written)
- musical note

- concerto
- nocturne
- dreamy
- waltz

- mazurka
- Polish
- report
- tsar

When he attended the Warsaw High School of Music, his teacher reported that Chopin was a musical genius. In fact, when Chopin played the piano for Alexander I, Tsar of Russia, it's reported the Tsar enjoyed his music so much that he gave the young musician a diamond ring.  This was when Chopin was only fifteen years old!

After completing school, he traveled to Europe. In 1829, Chopin

took a short trip to Vienna, Austria, where many other composers of the Romantic Era performed. He wanted to become more involved with the European music scene to establish his reputation and perhaps become famous.

At the young age of twenty years, he gave two performances at the Kärtnertortheater, a prominent theater in Vienna. The audience loved his *Variations, op. 2* on a Mozart theme and his *Rondo à la Krakowiak, op. 14.* Critics called him a genius of the piano. As a result, his *Variations, op. 2* was published by a Viennese music producer. This was the first of Chopin's music published outside of Warsaw.

**KEY WORDS**

- **take a trip** (take-took-taken)
- involve
- music scene
- establish
- reputation

- audience
- op.
- rondo
- critic
- as a result

- publish
- producer
- outside of

He went home to Poland and continued writing music and performing. Some of the pieces he wrote between 1829 and 1839 were études. The word étude means "a study." He wrote the études as practice or study of specific piano skills. Today, music students around the world still practice the études of Chopin. He wrote twenty-seven of these études. They were divided into three groups.

The most famous of the études in the first group is Op. 10, no. 3, sometimes called *Tristesse* meaning sadness, or *L'Adieu* meaning farewell. A famous étude from the second group is Op. 25, no. 1. It is also called *Aeolian Harp* and mimics the sound of a harp playing. The third group of études were written as part of a piano instruction book. They are called the *Trois Nouvelles Études* which means "three new studies."

▲ aeolian harp

(It is a musical instrument that has more than six strings and makes a sound by using wind. It originated with the god of wind, Aiolos, according to Greek mythology.)

(By Simon Speed (Own work) [CC0], via Wikimedia Commons)

**KEY WORDS**

- study
- divide into
- farewell
- aeolian harp
- mimic
- instruction

Beginning in 1829, he wrote two concertos for piano and orchestra, one in F Minor and one in E Minor. He had feelings for a soprano singer, and the Piano Concerto No. 2 in F Minor reflects those feelings.

The governor of the Grand Duchy of Poznan admired Chopin's music, and invited him to come and perform in Berlin. However, Chopin thought he could continue his success and increase his reputation better in Vienna. At the end of 1830, Chopin decided to return to Vienna with a friend. He gave a farewell concert in the National Theater in Warsaw. He played his Concerto in E Minor and the soprano singer who he loved sang.

Chopin traveled to Vienna, but just days after he arrived, Poland went to war with Russia. Chopin's friend went back to Warsaw to join the army, but Chopin stayed in Vienna. When Russia captured Warsaw, many Polish citizens escaped to Paris, France. The people who left Poland for political reasons were called émigrés.

Chopin also went to Paris and did what he could to help his fellow countrymen. He played at charity concerts to raise money for the Polish émigrés. He organized other fundraising events. While he was doing this, he became friends with some well-known Romantic Era composers and performers, such as Franz Liszt and Hector Berlioz. His reputation grew in Paris. Publishing companies in Paris, France, Leipzig, Germany, and London, England published his music.

**KEY WORDS**

- have a feeling for
- governor
- grand duchy
- Poznan
- increase

- go to war
- capture
- citizen
- escape
- émigré

- fellow countryman
- organize
- fundraising
- Leipzig

Chopin did not like to perform for large crowds, preferring to play the piano for a small audience. This is because much of his music was written just for piano, so it sounded best in a small hall rather than a concert hall. People loved his music because it was so light and thoughtful and reflected many different emotions. They called him the poet of the piano. Chopin once wrote, "Put all your soul into it, play the way you feel!" Today, experts say that Chopin's compositions were responsible for our modern piano technique.

During his time in Paris, Chopin deliberately disobeyed the Tsar of Russia and did not extend his passport. This made him a political refugee in France. It meant he could never go home to Warsaw to see his friends and family. Instead, he only saw them during holidays outside of Poland. They met in Germany and other places.

**POP QUIZ**

What did Chopin write about playing music?
ⓐ Put all your soul into it, play the way you feel!
ⓑ Something strange is happening with this symphony!

**KEY WORDS**

- crowd
- prefer
- rather than
- thoughtful

- expert
- be responsible for
- deliberately
- disobey

- extend
- refugee

Chopin had a hectic schedule of teaching music, traveling, and performing. This made him sick sometimes. When he proposed marriage to a young woman named Maria, her parents said they would only approve if he took better care of his health. That winter he fell ill, and Maria's parents broke off the engagement.

They did not think he could care for Maria, since he had so much trouble caring for himself. Chopin was hurt and saddened by this. He bundled all of her letters together and labeled them, "My sorrow."

**KEY WORDS**

- hectic
- propose marriage to
- approve
- take care of
- fall ill
- break off the engagement (break-broke-broken)

- have trouble + *Verb*-ing
- care for
- sadden
- bundle
- label
- sorrow

▲ George Sand

He took a trip to London in 1837 to try to forget about Maria. There he met a woman named Amantine Lucile Aurore Dupin. You may know her as the author George Sand. 🌐 He spent some time with her in Majorca, Spain. During their stay in Majorca, Chopin became ill with what may have been tuberculosis, a serious disease that affects the lungs. After that, they stayed in Nohant, France, where the weather was better for his lungs. He composed his most famous music during the years he spent with Sand in France. They lived as a couple until 1847, but then they parted. This depressed Chopin, and he almost completely gave up composing music. From 1847 until his death, he wrote very little music.

KEY WORDS

- **forget** (forget-forgot-forgotten)
- Majorca
- tuberculosis
- lung
- Nohant
- part

- **depress** (cf. depressed)
- **give up** (give-gave-given)
- convince
- go on a concert tour
- take a toll
- Guildhall

In April 1848, one of Chopin's students convinced him to go on a concert tour, including the castles of Scotland. Although he had been feeling better, this tour took a toll on his health. The cold, wet weather in Scotland was not good for his lungs. In November 1848, he did his last performance in London. It was a concert for Polish émigrés at the Guildhall in London. After that, he was too sick ever to perform again.

▲ the Guildhall in London

Chopin, the poet of the piano, died of tuberculosis on October 17, 1849. The music at his funeral included some of his own compositions, "Funeral March" from the Piano Sonata No. 2 and Prelude No. 4 in E Minor, as well as Prelude No. 6 in B Minor. He lived most of his life in France, but he never stopped caring

▲ the Holy Cross Church in Warsaw where Chopin's heart is buried

for his homeland of Poland. In fact, he loved Poland so much that he asked to have his heart buried in Warsaw, Poland. Chopin's sister took his heart back to Warsaw and placed it in an urn in the Holy Cross Church. So while his physical heart is in Poland, the rest of his body is buried in France. Frédéric Chopin could never go back to Warsaw while he was alive, but his heart now rests in his beloved homeland.

Chopin's grave in Paris, France ▶

**KEY WORDS**

- prelude
- as well as
- urn
- Holy Cross Church
- beloved

# Comprehension Quiz

**A** Fill in each blank with the right word(s) below.

| folk music    engagement    Russia    a diamond ring |
| --- |

❶ After hearing Chopin's music, Tsar Alexander I of Russia gave
  him _____.

❷ Maria's parents broke off the _____ when Chopin became
  ill.

❸ Soon after Chopin went to Vienna, Poland went to war with
  _____.

❹ In the years 1823 to 1826, when Chopin spent summer holidays
  in the country, he wrote down the songs and musical notes of
  _____.

**B** Mark T for true or F for false.

❶ Chopin wrote twenty-seven études.  T F

❷ *Tristesse* is the name of one of the most famous études.  T F

❸ Students do not play études today because they are
  old-fashioned.  T F

**C** Choose the best answer to each question.

**❶** What was the first piece of Chopin's music that was published by a Viennese publisher?

a) *Variations, op. 2* on a Mozart theme

b) *Rondo à la Krakowiak, op. 14*

c) *Trois Nouvelles Études*

d) *Tristesse*

**❷** Why did Chopin ask to have his heart buried in Warsaw, Poland, even though he had not lived there for many years?

a) His parents were still living there.

b) He never stopped loving his homeland.

c) Polish émigrés insisted he be buried in Warsaw.

d) He did not want France to be his final resting place.

**❸** What unusual thing happened to Chopin's body after he died?

a) His body was put in a glass coffin.

b) The Tsar of Russia placed a diamond ring in Chopin's coffin.

c) His body was buried in one place, and his heart was buried in another.

d) He was buried in one place, but then they moved his body to a new grave.

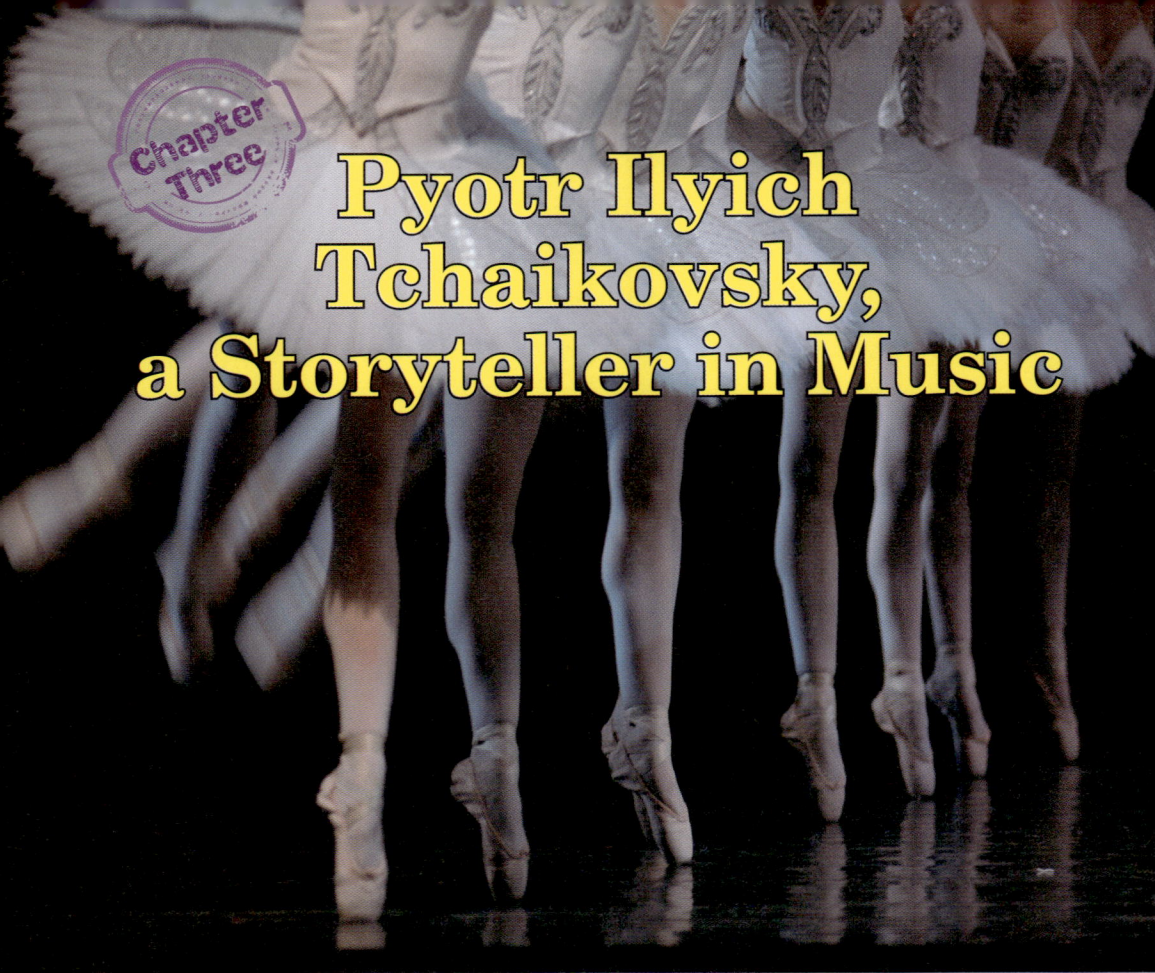

# Pyotr Ilyich Tchaikovsky, a Storyteller in Music

One of the most popular Russian composers of all time is Pyotr Ilyich Tchaikovsky. Have you ever hummed the *Dance of the Sugar Plum Fairy* from the ballet *The Nutcracker*? Then you know one of the compositions written by Tchaikovsky. He also wrote the music for other famous ballets, such as *Swan Lake, Romeo and Juliet*, and *The Sleeping Beauty*. His ballets and much of his music tells beloved stories.

Tchaikovsky was born on May 7, 1840 in Russia. His father worked as a mine inspector and metal works manager. Like Chopin, Tchaikovsky began taking piano lessons when he was very young. When he was four years old, he wrote his first song, and when he was five, he began taking piano lessons. Some of the musical pieces he practiced were Frédéric Chopin's mazurkas!

▲ Pyotr Ilyich Tchaikovsky

▲ a scene from *The Nutcracker*

**KEY WORDS**

- storyteller
- hum
- sugar plum

- fairy
- ballet
- nutcracker

- mine
- inspector
- metal works

Tchaikovsky's parents did not want him to choose music as a career. They wanted him to work for the civil service. When he was nineteen years old, he did take a job with the Ministry of Justice to make his father happy, but Tchaikovsky's heart was in music, not government. Through his teen years and into his twenties, Tchaikovsky took music lessons. He attended the Russian Musical Society, and when the St. Petersburg Conservatory opened, he was one of the school's first composition students. While taking lessons, he grew to appreciate Mozart's music and Italian music. Once he knew he wanted to spend his life devoted to beautiful music, he resigned from his position with the Ministry of Justice.

**POP QUIZ**

What did Tchaikovsky's parents want him to choose as a career?

ⓐ They wanted him to go into the civil service.
ⓑ They wanted him to be a writer.

## KEY WORDS

- civil service
- the Ministry of Justice
- government
- Russian Musical Society
- St. Petersburg
- conservatory
- grow to + *Verb* (grow-grew-grown)
- appreciate
- once

- devote to
- resign
- graduate
- voyevoda
- follow up A with B
- debut
- disaster
- drop
- iconic

Tchaikovsky graduated in December of 1865, and then he moved to Moscow to teach music at the Moscow Conservatory. During the next ten years, he wrote his first symphony, Symphony No. 1 in G Minor, and also his first opera, *The Voyevoda*. He followed up those works with more symphonies, operas, and concertos. In 1875, he finished the ballet, *Swan Lake*. The debut performance of *Swan Lake* in February 1877 was a disaster, and the theater dropped it. Today, *Swan Lake* is an iconic ballet and is a favorite all around the world!

In the summer of 1877, Tchaikovsky married one of his music students, a young woman named Antonina Milyukova. He immediately knew it was a mistake, and a few weeks later, he left the country and never returned to his wife. This made him sad and depressed, but he continued to write beautiful music. A wealthy widow of a railroad tycoon named Nadezhda von Meck greatly admired his work. She contacted Tchaikovsky and offered to pay him a monthly allowance if he would continue to write music. However, she made one requirement: Tchaikovsky must never meet her! He agreed, and the generosity of his mysterious benefactor allowed him to quit teaching and devote himself full time to composing new music. During this time, he wrote his famous *1812 Overture*.

**KEY WORDS**

- widow
- railroad
- tycoon
- monthly
- allowance
- requirement
- generosity
- benefactor
- overture

The Tsar of Russia, Alexander III, and his family enjoyed Tchaikovsky's music. Alexander III hired Tchaikovsky to write the music for the imperial coronation in 1883. After that, he awarded the composer a lifetime allowance and a valuable ring as a personal gift from the tsar. In addition, when Tchaikovsky died, Alexander III gave him a state funeral, a high honor reserved for very important people.

**KEY WORDS**
- coronation
- award
- valuable
- in addition
- a state funeral
- reserve for

Now that Tchaikovsky had no worries about money, he retired to a country home in 1885 in a place called Klin, near Moscow, Russia. Each morning he read books and took walks in the forest. In the afternoons, he composed music. In the evenings, he entertained friends and played piano duets with them. It was a luxurious life, paid for by Nadezhda von Meck.

In December of 1887, when he was 47 years old, he set out on his first European concert tour. He had great success, so he embarked on a second European tour in 1888, and visited many new cities. While he was doing this, he wrote the ballet *The Sleeping Beauty*. In another burst of inspiration in 1890, he wrote an opera called *The Queen of Spades* in just forty-four days! 🌐

▲ a scene from *The Queen of Spades*

### KEY WORDS

- now that
- retire
- Klin
- entertain

- luxurious
- set out (set-set-set)
- embark on
- burst (burst-burst-burst)

- run out (run-ran-run)
- afford

Meck had been giving Tchaikovsky an allowance now for fourteen years, but her money was running out. She wrote to him and told him she could not afford to send him any more money. This deeply saddened Tchaikovsky, because even though he didn't need her money, she had become an important friend to him. They had never met, but they had written hundreds of letters to each other. In the letters, Tchaikovsky called Meck his best friend.

▲ Carnegie Hall

In 1891, Tchaikovsky traveled to New York City for the grand opening of Carnegie Hall where he performed his *Coronation March*. While in America, he went on tour to Washington D.C., Baltimore, Philadelphia, Niagara Falls, and Buffalo. When he returned to Russia, he finished the opera *Iolanta* and the ballet *The Nutcracker*. 🌐 *The Nutcracker* used a brand new instrument of the time called the celesta. It makes a magical, tinkling sound. It is what you hear when you listen to the *Dance of the Sugar Plum Fairy*. *Hedwig's Theme*, the music in the opening of the *Harry Potter* films also uses the celesta because of its magical quality.

**KEY WORDS**

- grand opening
- Carnegie Hall
- go on tour
- brand new
- of the time
- magical
- tinkling

Tchaikovsky became world famous performing his music on his European tours to Leipzig, Berlin, Paris, and London, many of the same cities Chopin visited. Tchaikovsky even received an honorary doctorate from the University of Cambridge in June 1893. That was quite an honor. Pyotr Ilyich Tchaikovsky truly was another musical genius of the Romantic Era.

During 1893, he wrote Symphony No. 6 in B Minor, also called *Pathétique*. Tchaikovsky conducted the first public performance of *Pathétique* on October 28, 1893 in St. Petersburg at the Russian Musical Society. The music has a serious tone that evokes strong emotions. Tchaikovsky felt it was one of his best works but the audience didn't seem to like it. He wrote to his publisher, "Something strange is happening with this symphony! It's not that it displeased, but it has caused some bewilderment. So far as I myself am concerned, I'm more proud of it than any of my other works."

## POP QUIZ

Which university awarded Tchaikovsky an honorary doctorate in 1893?

ⓐ Cambridge
ⓑ Oxford

**KEY WORDS**

- honorary doctorate
- Pathétique
- evoke
- displease

- bewilderment
- so far as I am concerned
- be proud of

Five days later, on November 2, he became ill with cholera, a disease caused by contaminated water. Cholera was an epidemic in St. Petersburg that year. He died four days later, on November 6, at age fifty-three, just nine days after performing *Pathétique*, one of his greatest works.

Tchaikovsky's sudden death came as a great shock to the music world. His famous symphony was performed in London and in Moscow in the following months. When the audiences heard the dark and melancholy music, they began to think that Tchaikovsky may have had a premonition, or forewarning, of his own death. People began to say he wrote *Pathétique* as his requiem. After this, more rumors began, and some people even said he may have taken poison and committed suicide. However, all of the newspaper accounts from 1893 stated complications from cholera as the cause of his death. In later years, researchers disproved the suicide rumors. Now we know that Tchaikovsky died of a terrible disease at the height of his life and his creativity.

Tchaikovsky's statue in Moscow ▶

**KEY WORDS**

- cholera
- contaminated
- epidemic
- come as a shock to
- melancholy

- premonition
- forewarning
- requiem
- commit suicide
- account

- complication
- disprove
- at the height of

ВЕЛИКОМУ РУССКОМУ
КОМПОЗИТОРУ
ПЕТРУ ИЛЬИЧУ
ЧАЙКОВСКОМУ

## POP QUIZ

**What did some people say about Tchaikovsky's death?**

ⓐ He died from cancer.

ⓑ He committed suicide by taking poison.

# Comprehension Quiz

**A** Fill in each blank with the right word(s) below.

| hated | mine inspector | cholera | European |
|---|---|---|---|

❶ Pyotr Ilyich Tchaikovsky's father worked as a _____.

❷ When *Swan Lake* was first performed in 1877, the audience _____ it.

❸ Tchaikovsky went on his first _____ tour when he was 47 years old.

❹ Tchaikovsky died of complications from _____.

**B** Mark T for true or F for false.

❶ Tchaikovsky studied at the Russian Musical Society and the Moscow Conservatory.    T   F

❷ Tchaikovsky's first symphony is Symphony No. 1 in G Minor.    T   F

❸ After returning to Russia from America, Tchaikovsky finished the ballet *The Nutcracker*.    T   F

❹ Another name for Symphony No. 6 in B Minor is *1812 Overture*.    T   F

**C** Choose the best answer to each question.

❶ Nadezhda von Meck placed an unusual requirement on Tchaikovsky when she agreed to give him an allowance. What was it?

a) All of his compositions had to be dedicated to her.

b) He could not marry anyone.

c) He had to perform the music for her before anyone else.

d) They could never meet in person.

❷ What famous ballet did Tchaikovsky compose during his second European tour?

a) *Swan Lake*                     b) *Romeo and Juliet*

c) *The Sleeping Beauty*           d) *The Nutcracker*

❸ Why did audiences think Tchaikovsky may have known his death was near?

a) He used to visit fortune tellers.

b) He was sick for a long time.

c) *Pathétique* had a dark and melancholy sound.

d) He was depressed.

# Sergei Rachmaninoff, the Composer Who Loved Bells

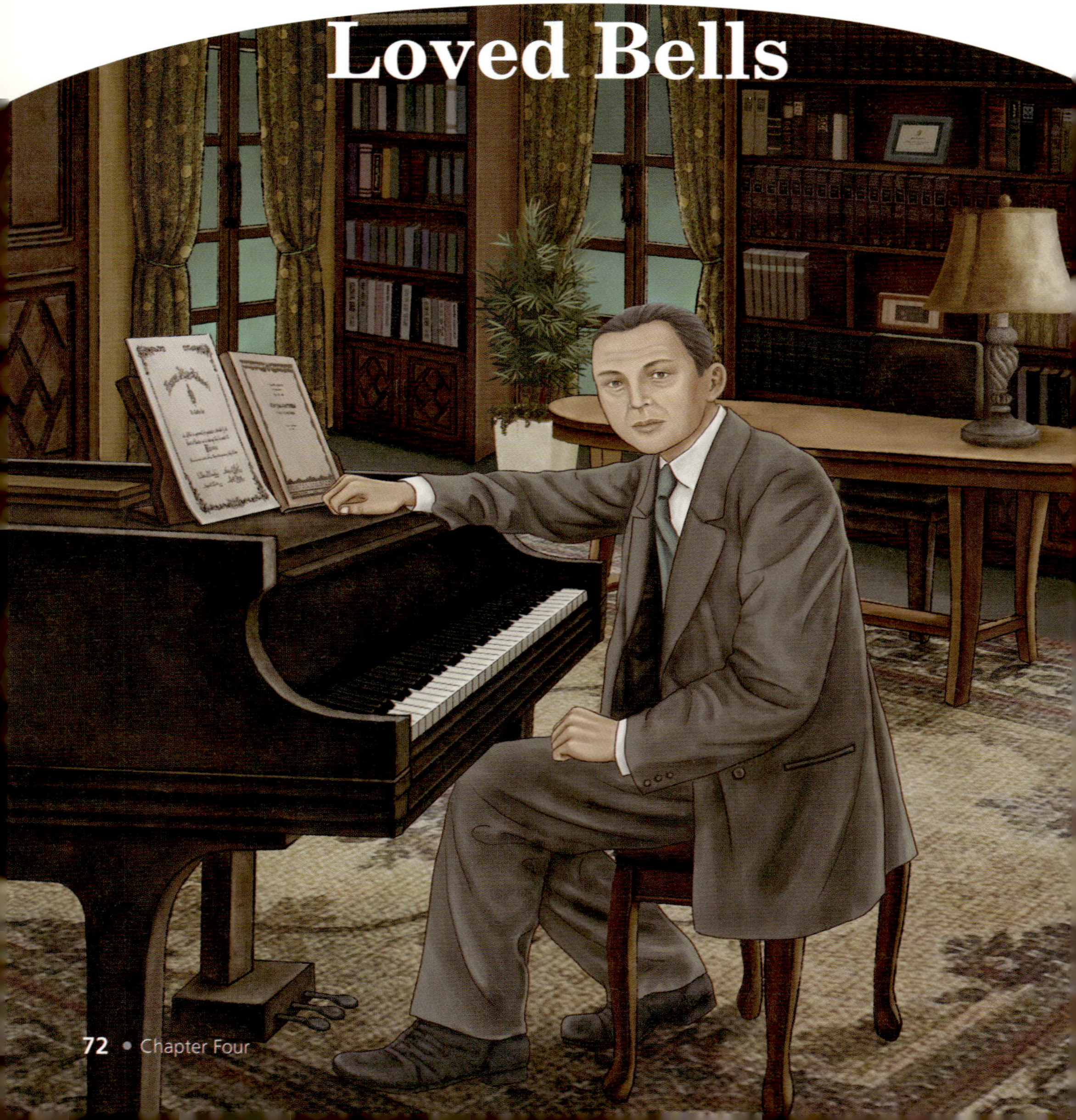

One of the last of the Romantic Era composers, Sergei Rachmaninoff was from Russia. Like other composers of this period, his music took him all around the world and he finally settled in Beverly Hills, California.

Sergei Rachmaninoff was born April 1, 1873, on his family's estate near Lake Ilmen in the Novgorod district of Russia. Rachmaninoff's family members were wealthy aristocrats. They owned five estates and were friends of very important people in Russia. His father was a retired army officer, and his mother was the daughter of a general. Even though Rachmaninoff began music lessons at age four, he was expected to serve in the army as an officer like his father. Then four tragedies happened that changed the course of his life.

Rachmaninoff's father liked to have parties and play games, including gambling games. He also invested money in risky businesses that went bad. Each time this happened, his father would sell some of their land or estates. But by 1882, Rachmaninoff's father had lost the last of the family fortune and they had to sell all of their estates. They moved to an apartment in St. Petersburg. This was the first tragedy.

**KEY WORDS**

- settle in
- Lake Ilmen
- Novgorod
- district
- army officer
- general
- serve
- tragedy
- gambling
- invest
- risky
- fortune

Rachmaninoff continued music lessons at the St. Petersburg Conservatory, the same school Tchaikovsky had attended! That same year, Rachmaninoff's sister Sofia died of diphtheria, a disease that attacks the mucus membranes and makes it difficult to swallow or breathe. 📖 This was the second tragedy. Before modern medicine, many people died of diphtheria, but now children are vaccinated to prevent this disease.

After his sister Sofia's death, Rachmaninoff's father felt so bad that he left the family and moved to Moscow. This was the third tragedy. In those days it was very hard for a woman without a husband to provide a home for her children.

## POP QUIZ

Mark T for true or F for false.

Rachmaninoff attended the same school as Tchaikovsky. **T / F**

### KEY WORDS

- diphtheria
- mucus
- membrane
- swallow
- medicine
- vaccinate

- provide a home for
- talented
- be set to + *Verb*
- Bolshoi Theater
- anemia
- oxygen

- cell
- get well
- fail
- step in
- take over
- Russian Orthodox Church

Rachmaninoff's other sister Yelena was a talented dancer. She was set to join the Bolshoi Theater, famous for ballet and opera. But she fell ill with anemia, a disease of the blood. Anemia prevents the blood from carrying oxygen to the cells, and makes a person extremely tired. Yelena could not get well, and she died. This was the fourth tragedy. All of this happened by 1885! You can imagine how depressed Sergei was. In fact, he began failing his classes in school. Fortunately, his grandmother stepped in to help. She took over his spiritual training, taking him to the Russian Orthodox Church. He loved the sounds of the bells during the services, and he later included them in much of his music.

▲ the bell tower in a Russian Orthodox monastery

When he began getting into more trouble at school, his cousin Alexander Siloti, decided to help. Siloti was a successful pianist and conductor, and he sent Sergei to the Moscow Conservatory, to be taught by a strict teacher named Nikolai Zverev. Without the discipline Rachmaninoff learned from this teacher, he might never have become such a great piano virtuoso. So we can thank Rachmaninoff's grandmother, cousin, and teacher for giving us the gift of his beautiful music!

While he was at the Moscow Conservatory, he wrote an opera called *Aleko*. When he graduated, he received a high honor for it called the Great Gold Medal. He also wrote a piece called Prelude in C-Sharp Minor that became very popular. For the rest of his life, people all around the world asked him to play it for them.

Rachmaninoff spent the summer of 1893 writing music, and in the fall he met Pyotr Ilyich Tchaikovsky. Rachmaninoff admired the famous Russian musician. They discussed working together, but first Rachmaninoff had to go to Kiev to conduct his opera *Aleko*. By the time he returned to Moscow, Tchaikovsky had suddenly died. Who knows what would have happened if the two great composers had worked together?

As it happened, in 1897, Rachmaninoff's Symphony No. 1 in D Minor had its debut and the audience hated it. Rachmaninoff was emotional and the harsh reviews made him so depressed he did not write any more music for three years. He saw a doctor who helped him get through this difficult time in his life. The first piece he wrote after this was the Piano Concerto No. 2 in C Minor, which he dedicated to his doctor. Rachmaninoff played it at a premiere in 1901 and the audience loved it. It is still popular today.

**KEY WORDS**

- conductor
- strict
- discipline
- virtuoso
- sharp (#)
- Kiev
- as it happens[happened]
- harsh
- review
- get through
- premiere

In 1902, he married Natalia Alexandrovna Satina. She was his cousin, but in those days, especially in the aristocracy, cousins were allowed to marry. They stayed married until his death forty-one years later. In 1904, he took a job as a conductor at the Bolshoi Theater, the same theater his sister Yelena had planned on joining. After two years, he resigned his position to have more time to write music. He went on tour in America in 1909 and became so popular that he was asked back for more tours. However, Rachmaninoff did not enjoy America as much as it enjoyed him. So back to Russia he went.

In 1913, he wrote a choral symphony called *The Bells*. It was based on a poem written by a Romantic Era American poet and author, Edgar Allan Poe.  His poem, *The Bells*, begins happily with tinkling sleigh bells. Then, in the next stanza, Poe writes about joyful wedding bells. The third stanza turns away from happiness and focuses on alarm bells. In the fourth and final stanza he writes about mourning bells played at a funeral. His poem describes the course of life from birth to the grave. Poe's writing often focused on death and the supernatural, a common theme in Romanticism. Rachmaninoff loved to include bells in his music, so Poe's four stanza poem was a perfect inspiration for the four movement choral symphony, *The Bells*.

▲ Edgar Allan Poe

**KEY WORDS**

- aristocracy
- sleigh bell
- stanza
- turn away from
- alarm bell
- mourning
- Romanticism
- movement

▲ a funeral for people who got killed by police during the Russian Revolution

In 1917, Russia had a revolution. The Russian people wanted to do away with the ruling tsar and to get rid of the aristocracy. Remember, Rachmaninoff and his family were part of the aristocracy. They had to run away to save their lives. They left Russia on a sled, only taking a few notebooks with Rachmaninoff's musical compositions in them. The family escaped to Scandinavia.

Rachmaninoff had more offers to work in the United States, so they moved to New York in 1918. Steinway, a company that manufactures musical instruments, gave him a piano that he used on his concert tours. He also signed a contract with the Victor Talking Machine, one of the first recording companies. Rachmaninoff was one of its exclusive artists and recorded his music with the company between 1920 and 1942.

**KEY WORDS**

- do away with
- ruling
- get rid of
- run away

- save
- sled
- Scandinavia
- manufacture

- contract
- exclusive

While Rachmaninoff was doing this, he became good friends with Vladimir Horowitz, a classical pianist young enough to be his son.  Horowitz greatly admired Rachmaninoff, and the two men enjoyed performing music together, both on the stage and at Rachmaninoff's home.

▲ Niccoló Paganini

All of these concerts and recordings in the United States didn't leave Rachmaninoff much time to compose. He solved that problem by building a home in Switzerland. Every year from 1932 to 1939, he spent summers in Switzerland, writing music. This is where he wrote *Rhapsody on a Theme of Paganini* in 1934, Symphony No. 3 in A Minor (op. 44) in 1935 and 1936, and began the *Symphonic Dances* (op. 45) for orchestra. Niccoló Paganini was a famous violinist and this piece was inspired by his music. After this, Rachmaninoff moved to Beverly Hills, and finished composing the *Symphonic Dances* in 1940.

**POP QUIZ**

Where did Rachmaninoff write *Rhapsody on a Theme of Paganini*?

ⓐ United States
ⓑ Switzerland

**KEY WORDS**

- rhapsody
- symphonic dance
- turn out
- melanoma
- cancer

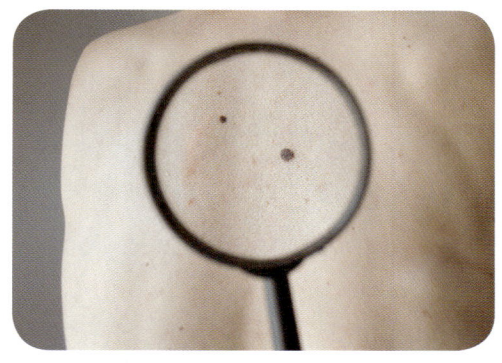

▲ melanoma on someone's back

On a concert tour in 1942 Rachmaninoff became ill. It turned out he had melanoma, which is a type of cancer. Rachmaninoff did not let cancer stop him from doing something important he wanted to do. He and his wife both took a test and became American citizens in February 1943. He gave his last performance on February 17, 1943. He must have known he didn't have long to live, because he chose to play Chopin's Piano Sonata No. 2, which includes "Funeral March" as the third movement. These are the same movements that were played at Chopin's funeral. Rachmaninoff died just over one month later, on March 28, 1943.

In addition to operas and piano concertos, Rachmaninoff also wrote a cappella for choirs. A cappella music is sung with no instruments except the human voice. Rachmaninoff wanted a cappella piece, *All-Night Vigil*, to be sung at his own funeral. He wanted to be buried in Switzerland, but since he died during World War II, he had to be buried in the United States. It was too difficult to send his body to his home in Switzerland during wartime.

Rachmaninoff's music is of the Romantic Era, but some pieces also sound modern, especially the music written in Switzerland during the 1930s after the Romantic Era had ended. He admired and was influenced by Mozart, Chopin, and Tchaikovsky. Just before he died, he wrote, "Music is enough for a lifetime, but a lifetime is never enough for music."

**POP QUIZ**

Mark T for true or F for false.

Rachmaninoff continued to write music even after the Romantic Era had ended.　T / F

**KEY WORDS**

- a cappella
- vigil
- wartime
- overcome (overcome-overcame-overcome)
- hardship

- recall
- overlap
- live through
- uprising
- hallmark

These four composers are all considered musical geniuses. All of them overcame hardships in their lives, but they didn't let that stop them from composing music. They also influenced each other. As you will recall, Schubert admired Beethoven, and was buried next to him. Tchaikovsky played Chopin's mazurkas. Rachmaninoff would have worked with Tchaikovsky if Tchaikovsky had lived long enough. The composers' lives overlapped and extended through the Romantic Era, the era of passion and change. The historical events they lived through, the revolutions, the wars, the uprisings, and the personal tragedies all influenced their music. Out of these experiences came music that created deep emotions and beauty, the hallmark of the Romantic Era.

# Chapter Four

# Comprehension Quiz

**A** These sentences are about the tragedies that happened to Rachmaninoff in his childhood. Put the sentences in order.

❶ Sofia died of diphtheria.

❷ Yelena died of anemia.

❸ Father moved to Moscow.

❹ They sold their estates and moved to an apartment in St. Petersburg.

_____ → _____ → _____ → _____

**B** Mark T for true or F for false.

❶ Rachmaninoff's wife, Natalia Alexandrovna Satina was also his cousin. 　T　F

❷ Rachmaninoff's father lost the family fortune through gambling and bad investments. 　T　F

❸ Alexander Siloti stepped in to help Sergei Rachmaninoff because Rachmaninoff got into trouble at church. 　T　F

❹ Diphtheria is a disease of the blood. 　T　F

**C** Choose the best answer to each question.

**❶** What did Sergei Rachmaninoff love about the Russian Orthodox Church services?

a) the chanting of the prayers

b) the calming smell of the incense

c) the lighting of the candles

d) the sounds of the bells

**❷** Why did Rachmaninoff stop composing music for three years?

a) He was busy getting married.

b) He was depressed because audiences hated his Symphony No. 1 in D Minor.

c) He had to take care of his sick mother.

d) He wanted to try a different type of work.

**❸** Why did Rachmaninoff need to escape from Russia?

a) It was the Russian Revolution and people wanted to kill all aristocrats.

b) Russia went to war with Poland and Rachmaninoff did not want to be in the army.

c) Rachmaninoff was sick and needed to find a better doctor.

d) Rachmaninoff's wife wanted to move to another country.

# Let's Review the Story

Fill in the blanks to review the story.

**Title:** Romantic Era [          ]

## Romantic Era

The major focus of the Romantic Era was universal  f [          ]
such as  l [          ] , anger, grief, sadness, and [          ] . Some of
the historical events that affected composers in this era were the
[  I          ] Revolution, the Russian Revolution, and the war
between Russia and [          ] , and other political and cultural
events.

## Each Composer

- Schubert (1797~1828) is remembered for  s [          ] quartets.
- Chopin (1810~1849) is remembered for  é [          ] .
- Tchaikovsky (1840~1893) is remembered for  b [          ] music
  for famous stories, such as *The Nutcracker* and *The Sleeping
  Beauty*.
- Rachmaninoff (1873~1943) is remembered for the use of
  [ be        ] in his music.

## Musical Compositions and Composers

- *Pathétique / Swan Lake*: [          ]
- *Études / Variations, op.* 2 on a Mozart theme: [          ]
- Symphony in C Major (The Great C Major) / "Ellens Gesang III":
  [          ]
- *Rhapsody on a Theme of Paganini / Aleko*: [          ]

# Let's Think & Talk

Think about the following questions and answer them freely.

❶ Arrange the characteristics of the composers and their musical works.

❷ Which composer in the book is your favorite? Why?

❸ Search in the book for the titles of musical works and then listen to them. Tell us which one is your favorite and why you chose it.

❹ Do you know any other composers in the Romantic Era? Search for information about their lives and musical works and let us know what you have found.

# Let's Review the Story

**Answers**

---

**Title:** Romantic Era   Composers

---

**Romantic Era**

The major focus of the Romantic Era was universal feelings such as love, anger, grief, sadness, and joy. Some of the historical events that affected composers in this era were the Industrial Revolution, the Russian Revolution, and the war between Russia and Poland, and other political and cultural events.

---

**Each Composer**

- Schubert (1797~1828) is remembered for string quartets.
- Chopin (1810~1849) is remembered for études.
- Tchaikovsky (1840~1893) is remembered for ballet music for famous stories, such as *The Nutcracker* and *The Sleeping Beauty*.
- Rachmaninoff (1873~1943) is remembered for the use of bells in his music.

---

**Musical Compositions and Composers**

- *Pathétique / Swan Lake*: Tchaikovsky
- *Études / Variations, op.* 2 on a Mozart theme: Chopin
- Symphony in C Major (The Great C Major) / "Ellens Gesang III": Schubert
- *Rhapsody on a Theme of Paganini / Aleko*: Rachmaninoff

## Smart Readers: **Wise** & **Wide**

# After-reading Test

- Romantic Era Composers
- Level 6
- 25 Questions

 (Vocabulary 5 / Reading Comprehension 16 /

 Sentence Structure & Grammar 4)

1. Which of the following pair has the wrong past tense form of the verb?
   ① deal – dealt
   ② bring – brought
   ③ throw – threw
   ④ overcome – overcome

2. Which of the following is NOT the word represents the feelings?
   ① depressed
   ② displeased
   ③ industrial
   ④ melancholic

3. Which of the following represents the rest of the words?
   ① cholera
   ② disease
   ③ melanoma
   ④ tuberculosis

4. What are the right words for the two blanks?

   > The Russian people wanted to do _____ with the ruling tsar
   > and to get rid _____ the aristocracy.

   ① to, from                    ② away, of
   ③ with, away                  ④ into, to

5. What is the common word for the two blanks?

> • Chopin almost completely gave _____ composing music.
> • He followed _____ those works with more symphonies, operas, and concertos.

① on                       ② of

③ up                       ④ into

6. Why is the Romantic Era of music an important period in music history?
   ① Very few famous composers lived then.
   ② All of the best classical music was written then.
   ③ During this time, many new forms of music were created.
   ④ It is not an important historical time period.

7. What is one thing that became much larger during the Romantic Era?
   ① the estates of aristocrats
   ② houses for working people
   ③ French horns
   ④ orchestras

8. What instruments were in Schubert's family string quartet?
   ① oboe, flute, French horn
   ② violin, viola, piano
   ③ violin, viola, oboe
   ④ violin, viola, violoncello

9. Schubert's friends held parties for him to promote his music. What were these parties called?
① Vienna Waltzes
② Austrian dinner parties
③ Schubertiades
④ The parties did not have a special name.

10. When Schubert played his own works for the first time at a concert in 1828, what composition did he play?
① *Rain in the Alps*
② *Dance by the Moonlight*
③ String Quartet in D Minor, D. 810
④ *Wind in the Trees*

11. Why is folk music important to Chopin's compositions?
① The music inspired his operas.
② The music inspired his symphonies.
③ The music inspired his mazurkas.
④ The music inspired his teachers.

12. How do the words, "play the way you feel" reflect the Romantic Era?
① Technique was not important to music of this era.
② The composer needed to ask audience members how they felt.
③ It was important to play an instrument that felt right to the musician.
④ The music of this era focused on feelings and emotions.

13. Choose two of the pieces that were played at Chopin's funeral.

① Funeral March

② Op. 25, no. 1

③ Prelude No. 4 in E Minor

④ *Rondo à la Krakowiak, op. 14*

14. For what historic event did Tsar Alexander III of Russia hire Tchaikovsky?

① the imperial coronation of 1883

② the baptism of the Tsarina in 1885

③ the funeral march for Tsar Alexander II of Russia

④ the end of the Russo−Turkish War

15. Why did Tchaikovsky come to New York City in 1891?

① to perform the *Coronation March* at the grand opening of Carnegie Hall

② to perform *Swan Lake* at the grand opening of Carnegie Hall

③ to perform Symphony No. 1 in G Minor at Cambridge

④ to perform *Pathétique* for the President of the United States

16. Why do you think the celesta, a brand new instrument of the time, was used in the performance of *The Nutcracker*?

① It makes a sound like nuts cracking.

② It has a tinkly, magical sound and *The Nutcracker* is a magical story.

③ Audiences were tired of hearing cymbals.

④ It makes a sound like toy soldiers marching.

17. What did Tchaikovsky write to his publisher regarding *Pathétique*?
    ① "I think I should start over on this piece."
    ② "Play the way you feel!"
    ③ "It is music for a lifetime."
    ④ "I'm more proud of it than any of my other works."

18. For which piece did Sergei Rachmaninoff win the Great Gold Medal when he graduated from school?
    ① *Aleko*
    ② Prelude in C-Sharp Minor
    ③ Piano Concerto No. 2 in C Minor
    ④ *The Bells*

19. What was the inspiration for Rachmaninoff's choral symphony written in 1913?
    ① *Lady of the Lake* by Walter Scott
    ② *Romeo and Juliet* by William Shakespeare
    ③ *Swan Lake* by Pyotr Ilyich Tchaikovsky
    ④ *The Bells* by Edgar Allan Poe

20. Which famous piece of music was written at Rachmaninoff's summer home in Switzerland?
    ① Prelude in C-Sharp Minor
    ② Symphony No. 1 in D Minor
    ③ *Rhapsody on a Theme of Paganini*
    ④ *The Bells*

21. What famous words did Rachmaninoff write near the end of his life?
    ① "Put all your soul into it, play the way you feel!"
    ② "Music is enough for a lifetime, but a lifetime is not enough for music."
    ③ "Something strange is happening with this symphony!"
    ④ "Ave Maria."

※ Choose the wrong part of each sentence. (22~24)

22.

Your teacher may <u>have had</u> you <u>practicing</u> with <u>a piece of</u> music
                  ①               ②            ③

<u>called</u> an étude.
  ④

23.

He <u>never thought</u> he could <u>be</u> <u>as</u> good a composer <u>so</u> the great
      ①                ② ③             ④

musician.

24.

He <u>became</u> good friends <u>with</u> Vladimir Horowitz, a classical pianist
   ①              ②

<u>enough young</u> <u>to be</u> his son.
   ③       ④

25. What is the correct sentence?
   ① So to Russia he back went.
   ② Back to Russia so he went.
   ③ So back to Russia he went.
   ④ So back to Russia went he.

# Memo

# Memo

Memo

# Memo

**Suzanne Pitner**

Suzanne Pitner is a teacher and writer who has enjoyed visiting Alaska, exploring Rome, teaching in China, and is looking forward to more world travel. She has a Master's Degree in Education, and is a graduate of the Long Ridge Writer's Group. In addition to writing educational articles and books, she writes historical fiction and contemporary fiction for young adults using the pen name Suzanne Lilly.

Smart Readers Wise & Wide 6-6

# Romantic Era Composers

Written by Suzanne Pitner
Illustrated by Mijeong Lee

First Published in September 2016

Editorial Manager: Juyon Choi
Editors: Kyunghee Jang, Jiyeong Park
Designer: Eunhee Lee
Cover Designer: Eunhee Lee

Published and distributed by

 Happy House

Darakwon Bldg., 64-1 Jandari-ro, Mapo-gu, Seoul, Korea 04031
Tel: 82-2-736-2031(ext. 250)    Fax: 82-2-732-2037
Homepage: www.ihappyhouse.co.kr
Publisher: Kyudo Chung

ISBN: 978-89-6653-413-5 18740 / 978-89-6653-156-1 18740(set)

[Components]
• 1 Audio CD (Recording Studio: Aram)
• Answer Keys & Korean Translation: Free download at www.ihappyhouse.co.kr